8/16

D0466484

NATIVE NATIONS OF THE
NORTHWEST COAST

BY ANITA YASUDA

The Child's World®

Published by The Child's World®
1980 Lookout Drive • Mankato, MN 56003-1705
800-599-READ • www.childsworld.com
Acknowledgments
The Child's World®: Mary Berendes, Publishing Director
Red Line Editorial: Editorial direction and production
The Design Lab: Design
Content Consultant: Dr. Majel Boxer, Chair and Assistant
Professor of Native American and Indigenous Studies, Fort
Lewis College

Photographs ©: Chris Miller/AP Images, cover, 2, 3 (bottom),
36–37; Marie-Lan Nguyen, 1, 34; Michael Penn/Juneau
Empire/AP Images, 3 (top), 6, 9, 10; Ted S. Warren/AP
Images, 3 (middle top), 16; Lissandra Melo/Shutterstock
Images, 3 (middle bottom), 21; Anna Abramskaya/
Shutterstock Images, 5; Arnold John Labrentz, Shutterstock
Images, 8; Frans Lanting/Corbis, 12; Chris Cheadle/All
Canada Photos/Corbis, 13; Library and Archives Canada,
PA-020921, 15; Werner Forman/Corbis, 17; Asahel Curtis, 19;
U.S. Fish and Wildlife Service, 22; Edward S. Curtis/Library
of Congress, 23; Robert Potts/Design Pics/Corbis, 24; H.
Ruckemann/UPI Photo Service/Newscom, 26; Max Herman/
Shutterstock Images, 28–29; Lisa Reese/Demotix/Corbis, 30;
Ron Wurzer/KRT/Newscom, 32–33

Copyright © 2016 by The Child's World®
All rights reserved. No part of this book may be
reproduced or utilized in any form or by any means
without written permission from the publisher.
ISBN: 9781634070331
LCCN: 2014959804
Printed in the United States of America
Mankato, MN
July, 2015
PA02269

ABOUT THE AUTHOR

Anita Yasuda is the author of more than 100 books for children. She enjoys writing biographies, chapter books, and books about science and social studies. Anita lives with her family and dog in Huntington Beach, California.

Tlingit, Tsimshian, and Haida Peoples put on a parade during Celebration, a three-day annual cultural festival.

TABLE OF CONTENTS

ARCTIC
OCEAN

GREENLAND

*Gulf of
Alaska*

PACIFIC

OCEAN

*Hudson
Bay*

CANADA

ATLANTIC

OCEAN

UNITED STATES

KEY

NORTHWEST COAST
NATIVE NATIONS

N
W   E
S

MEXICO

*Gulf of
Mexico*

CHAPTER ONE

NORTHWEST COAST NATIVE NATIONS

The Northwest Coast region of North America extends from southern Alaska to Oregon. The area is known for its natural beauty. Lying to the west is the Pacific Ocean and many islands offshore. To the east are the Cascade, Olympic, Coast, and Rocky Mountains. This area has large lakes and major rivers, such as the Columbia.

The Cascade Mountains are surrounded by thick forests.

Thick forests of fir, cedar, and spruce cover much of the land. The climate is wet and mild.

For thousands of years, Native Peoples have lived in the Northwest. Dozens of **nations** call this area home, including the Tlingit, Makah, Haida, Chinook, Nisga'a, Puyallup, Tsimshian, and Nuu-chah-nulth. Each nation has its own **oral history** explaining how it came to be in the region. Language, knowledge, and ways of life developed and were shaped by each group's location. The climate and geography of the Northwest, rich with natural resources, helped each nation thrive. They developed their own distinct cultures and traditions.

The oceans and rivers of the Northwest teemed with fish. Native Peoples harvested shellfish and sea mammals. The annual **salmon run** was a major food source. People

Nations such as the Tlingit sponsor children's education in traditional ways of life, including outdoor skills.

preserved this fish for times when food was scarce. They also hunted animals such as deer and elk. They gathered plants, roots, and berries. Forests supplied materials for clothing, tools, and homes. Giant red cedars were used to build canoes. Water routes allowed Native Peoples to travel to trade and hunt.

Today, some Native Peoples of the Northwest live on **reservations** on or near their original lands. Each nation has a government that oversees it. Governments also watch over the nations' natural resources. In the Northwest, these resources include fisheries, timber, and mineral deposits. Nation governments also have their own courts and police forces. At school, children learn their nation's history, hear their language, and celebrate their culture.

The first people to live in the Northwest cut images of people, animals, spirals, and other geometric shapes into large rocks. These images are called **petroglyphs**. One of the best-known images is "She Who Watches." It shows a face overlooking the Columbia River.

CHAPTER TWO

TLINGIT

Totem poles welcome all to the Tlingit visitor center in Hoonah, Alaska.

Many Tlingit live below the Coast Mountains in the city of Juneau, Alaska. Sitka, Ketchikan, and Anchorage also have large Tlingit populations. Forests with deer, rivers with salmon, and seas with porpoises make southeast Alaska a rich land.

Few people speak Tlingit today. Teacher Linda Belarde created flash cards to help new speakers learn the language.

In the 19th century, a Tlingit group settled in Canada. Its descendants now live in Atlin, British Columbia, and Teslin, Yukon. Canadian Native Peoples are known as **First Nations**.

The Tlingit People once relied on the waters and forests for food and shelter. Traders came from Russia, Great Britain, and the United States in the late 1700s. Tlingit began to trade pelts for goods such as tobacco. Then the United States took possession of Alaska from Russia in 1867. The Tlingit lost much of their land. Under

SAY IT			
	beach	e'ek	(e-k-tuh)
	dog	keitl	(keyk)
	blueberry	kanata-a'	(kuh-n-yah-tah)
	eagle	ch-'aak	(chawk)

People carry a canoe ashore during Celebration 2012. Canoeists traveled the coast of southeast Alaska to open the festival.

federal law, Alaska Natives including the Tlingit did not have the same rights as other U.S. citizens. They tried for years unsuccessfully to claim their lands.

The Alaska Native Claims Settlement Act (ANCSA) was a step toward correcting the past. Tlingit and other Alaskan Natives reached a cash and land agreement with the U.S. government in 1971. The act created corporations of which each Alaska Native owns a part. One is Sealaska Corporation, owned by the Tlingit and Haida in Juneau. It is one of the top employers in southeast Alaska. This is important because Tlingit face high rates of unemployment. Jobs in small Alaskan towns are few. Tourism is helping change this. Tlingit in Hoonah, Alaska, made an old salmon cannery into a popular tourism center. The Tlingit People also own gold mining, fishing, and timber corporations.

The sound of drums signals that Celebration has begun. Celebration is a Tlingit, Haida, and Tsimshian cultural festival. The Sealaska Heritage Institute puts it on every two years. Celebration is one of the largest events in Alaska. Participants dance in colorful traditional dress, some wearing masks. Thousands of people come to share their culture with others.

CHAPTER THREE

NUU-CHAH-NULTH

Nuu-chah-nulth artist Joe David creates a wood carving.

British explorer James Cook called the people who lived on Cape Flattery and the west coast of Vancouver Island the Nootka. Since 1978, they have gone by the name Nuu-chah-nulth. It means "all along the mountains." Today the term describes 14 related nations. Their territory once stretched from Cape Scott on Vancouver Island to Ozette Lake in Washington. Some Nuu-chah-nulth People live on reservations on Vancouver Island and the Olympic **Peninsula**. Tourism is one source of jobs, but most people work in fishing.

Early Nuu-chah-nulth People also relied on the seas and rivers. They fished for salmon, halibut, and cod. Tidal waters provided them with abalone, shellfish, and sea urchins. They traveled by canoe to trade and hunt. Water is once again playing an important role for the nation. The Nuu-chah-nulth Tribal Council now runs **hydroelectric** plants near Port Alberni, Vancouver Island. The plants create many jobs.

The council is also working to gain better control of logging on their land. The

Nuu-chah-nulth craftspeople weave cedar bark into baskets.

Nuu-chah-nulth People believe cedar trees were a gift from the Creator. In the past, cedar bark was turned into baskets and clothing. It was split into boards for homes. Some homes were nearly 100 feet (30 m) long.

From the mid-1700s, the Nuu-chah-nulth came into contact with European fur traders and explorers. For the next hundred years, more settlers came. Settlers did not understand Native culture. By the 19th century, the U.S. and Canadian federal governments wanted all Native Peoples, including the Nuu-chah-nulth, to adopt Euro-American beliefs and culture. Governments set up **residential schools** to speed up this process. Many children were forced to attend government-funded boarding schools. They left home and went far from their families. The conditions were terrible.

Many children suffered years of abuse. The schools aimed to erase Native culture. Children were punished for speaking their first languages. The governments made many children attend residential schools until the middle of the 20th century. A few boarding schools are still open in the United States. But today they teach Native cultures and histories.

In 2012, a member from the nation helped to create a language app with words and phrases. Nuu-chah-nulth language classes are taught at some local schools.

Ha-Shilth-Sa is a Nuu-chah-nulth word meaning "interesting news." It is also the name of Canada's oldest First Nations newspaper, the *Ha-Shilth-Sa*. The paper was first published in 1974. It reports on Nuu-chah-nulth news. It also presents other Canadian news from a First Nations perspective.

A residential school in Regina, Saskatchewan, 1908

The Nuu-chah-nulth Tribal Council also runs summer programs for children. Identifying plants and learning about cedar weaving are ways to continue traditional skills. There is also a strong marine science program. Leaders hope that more Nuu-chah-nulth children will pursue jobs in science.

CHAPTER FOUR

MAKAH

The Makah call themselves *Kwih-dich-chuh-ahtx*. This means "people who live by the rocks and seagulls." The Makah People once lived in five villages on the rocky coast of the Olympic Peninsula. The villages were called Bahaada, Deah (now called Neah

Makah canoeists paddle in Tribal Journey 2005, an event in Washington featuring several Native Nations.

A Makah basket lid shows a whale hunt.

Bay), Waatch, Sooes, and Ozette. Treaties with the U.S. government in the 19th century ended in the Makah giving up much of their land. Today, the Makah have a reservation on the peninsula. It has thick evergreen forests and sandy beaches. The 48-square-mile (124 sq km) reservation has a health clinic and public schools. More than 90 percent of the children in the elementary school have Makah heritage. Makah culture and traditions are an important part of their studies. Two classes per week focus on Makah language and culture. Children may hear oral histories or build model **longhouses**.

Approximately 2,300 Makah live on the reservation. Yearly events such as the Annual Makah Days bring the community together for canoe races, traditional food, and games. A tribal government with five elected members runs the reservation. The government passes laws and manages natural resources important to the nation's economy. The fishing village of Neah Bay is the center of the community. Many Makah work there. Many visitors come to fish during the summer. The Makah also farm trout and other fish.

The Makah Nation has long built its life around the sea. The Makah traditional diet includes fish, and they have also hunted whales. The Makah People tell of the first whale hunter, a **thunderbird**. It swooped down to catch a whale to feed the hungry people. Historically, not everyone could go on a whale hunt. It was an honor passed down through families. It had to be earned. Hunters prayed and fasted before they sailed on large seagoing canoes.

More than 500 years ago, a mudslide buried the ancient Makah whaling village at Ozette. People are thought to have lived there for more than 3,000 years. In 1970, **archaeologists** worked with the Makah to excavate the site. Together they found six longhouses and more than 55,000 artifacts. There were **harpoons**, paddles, and baskets.

Makah whale hunt, 1910

The Makah stopped hunting whales in the 1920s. The whale population was very low then. Commercial hunters had killed too many of the animals. But beginning in 1994, the species of whale the Makah hunted was no longer endangered. The Makah then wanted to begin their traditional hunt again.

The International Whaling Commission recognized the right of the Makah to hunt whales. Despite protests by environmental groups, on May 17, 1999, members of the nation killed a gray whale for the first time in 70 years.

CHAPTER FIVE

HAIDA

The traditional home of the Haida People is the Haida Gwaii ("the islands of the people"). This string of islands lies in British Columbia, Canada, and southeastern Alaska. Today, Haida who live on the islands live mostly in small fishing villages.

A sculpture by Haida artist Bill Reid was displayed in the Vancouver, British Columbia, airport.

But most First Nations Haida do not live on Haida Gwaii. Instead, they live on the mainland.

Haida artisans have long been known for their cedar woodwork. Haida use trees for cultural purposes such as building canoes. They need special permission from the British Columbian government to use the cedars.

Galleries and museums around the world collect works by major Haida artists. A sculpture by Haida artist Bill Reid was on the Canadian 20 dollar bill from 2004 to 2012. The same sculpture welcomes people to the Canadian Embassy in Washington, DC. In 2014, Haida artist Robert Davidson recorded a video about Haida art at the Penn Museum in Philadelphia, Pennsylvania. His video helps students learn more about Haida carving.

The Haida People are also working to manage their natural resources. They want to support their people and keep the environment healthy. The nation owns a fish processing plant called Haida Wild. It has also invested in a wind energy farm. In Alaska, the Haida and the Tlingit own Sealaska Corporation. It sponsors summer language workshops. The Haida language is also taught in some Pacific Coast public schools with large Haida populations.

Haida artisans craft elaborate totem poles. The poles are usually made from red cedar. It is soft to carve. Its special oils keep it from rotting quickly. Poles have figures of animals, birds, and fish. Designs are passed down through families. Artist Robert Davidson raised one of the first modern totem poles on Haida Gwaii in 1969. New totem poles created on the island keep this important tradition alive.

CHAPTER SIX

CHINOOK

The Chinook People live in the states of Washington and Oregon. They once lived along the Columbia River and along Willapa Bay. Like all Native Peoples, many Chinook died from diseases after contact with Europeans. They had no **immunity** to

The Cathlapotle Plankhouse was built in the Chinook style in 2005.

Many Chinook joined other nations at the turn of the 20th century.

illnesses such as smallpox. Millions of Native Peoples died from disease by the end of the 19th century.

Disease killed so many Chinook that villages were abandoned. Many survivors married into other nations. This experience is common to many Native Peoples.

Today some Chinook live on the Quinault Indian Nation reservation in the state of Washington. The reservation is home to seven nations: the Quinault, Queet, Quileute, Hoh, Chehalis, Chinook, and Cowlitz Peoples. The reservation has its own government. It is one of the largest employers in Grays Harbor County.

Chinook who did not settle on the reservation formed the Chinook Nation. Five groups make up the Chinook Nation. They are the Cathlamet, Clatsop, Lower Chinook, Wahkiakum, and Willapa. The federal government does not recognize it as a nation. A federally recognized nation has a relationship such as a treaty with the government. These **sovereign** nations govern

A cement copy of a burial canoe honors Comcomly, one of the Chinook leaders who met U.S. explorers Meriwether Lewis and William Clark during their 1804–1809 trip.

themselves, run their economies, and decide their membership. Federally recognized nations also benefit from federal programs. In 2009, U.S. Representative Brian Baird asked Congress for the Chinook Nation to be recognized. This bill did not pass, and the struggle for recognition continues.

The First Salmon Ceremony is a longstanding Chinook tradition. It shows respect for nature by thanking the salmon for the food they provide. In 2013, the Chinook Indian Nation Tribal Council started a new way to honor tradition. Members set out in canoes down the Lower Columbia River. Along the way they stayed with different Chinook families as their ancestors once did. In the past, the Chinook were known as traders. The traders skillfully navigated the rapids and cascades of the Columbia River.

They stocked their canoes with food and items to trade, such as clothing and baskets.

In the 19th century, the Chinook developed a language for trade called Chinuk Wawa. It uses a few Chinook words, other Native words, and English. Today children and adults learn Chinuk Wawa at the Grand Ronde Reservation in Oregon.

SAY IT

one	ixt	(ikt)
two	môkst	(mokst)
three	Łun	(klone)
man	man	(man)
woman	Łóóc man	(klootch-man)

CHAPTER SEVEN

NISGA'A

Nisga'a members celebrate a treaty signing with the British Columbian government.

British Columbia's Nass Valley has been home to the Nisga'a people for uncounted generations. The Nass Valley is rich in natural resources, from thick forests to the Nass River. Nisga'a oral history explains the origin of these resources. The Nisga'a tell of a supreme being who sends Raven to help the people. Raven creates everything the nation needs to live.

Early Nisga'a relied on salmon for food. They collected **eulachon** fish for their oil. Other Northwest nations such as the Tlingit traded with the Nisga'a for it. The forests provided the Nisga'a with cedar. They wove the soft inner bark of cedar trees into waterproof clothing, including basket-shaped hats.

Like other Northwest nations, Nisga'a traditional life was threatened beginning in the 1860s. Nonnative people, including

The Nisga'a use a code of laws and customs called the *Ayuukhl Nisga'a*. The laws have been passed down orally since ancient times. They tell how certain actions are rewarded or punished. Some explain marriage or divorce. Others talk about the origins of the Nisga'a.

loggers and farmers, arrived then. For more than 100 years, the Nisga'a struggled for land rights. Then, on May 11, 2000, a treaty with the British Columbian government took effect. It gave back 772 square miles (2,019 sq km) of public land to the Nisga'a. The Nisga'a own all forest resources and mineral rights on their land, including oil. They run a salmon conservation program.

Thank you!	T'ooyaksiẏ ńiin!	(toi-yak-si-neen)
How are you doing?	Aam wilaa wilina?	(aan-wila-wil-ina)
I am doing fine.	Aam wilaa wiliẏ	(aan-wila-wil-ah)
Wait for me.	Ji gibayin ńiiẏ!	(jis-g-bai-yun-nih)

SAY IT

Power plants and dams built along waterfalls and rivers produce electricity. The Nisga'a earn money from these hydroelectric projects.

More than 6,000 people belong to the Nisga'a Nation. They are divided into four *pdeek*, similar to tribes or clans. They are Raven, Killer Whale, Wolf, and Eagle. Children become part of their mothers' *pdeek*. The Nisga'a Museum highlights the nation's culture. A Nisga'a longhouse and traditional bowl inspired the design. The museum has shown work by Nisga'a artist Norman Tait. Tait is a master carver of wood and metal. One of his totem poles stands in front of the Field Museum in Chicago, Illinois.

Norman Tait's totem pole stands outside the Field Museum in Chicago.

CHAPTER EIGHT

PUYALLUP

The Puyallup Nation is one of the largest in Washington State. It has more than 4,000 members. A seven-member elected council leads the nation. The council chairman represents the Puyallup to the state and federal governments.

The Puyallup Nation has hosted a yearly powwow for more than 30 years.

The Puyallup People are building environmentally friendly housing projects. In 2013, they built a housing complex called the Place of Hidden Water. Its design was inspired by a longhouse. Builders used recycled and green building materials. Rainwater filters through a rain garden.

Once, the Puyallup lived in small villages along Puget Sound and on southern Vashon Island. Some Puyallup still live there. The nation has a reservation in Tacoma, Washington. From the 1830s, the U.S. government under President Andrew Jackson began to force Native Peoples off their lands. The government wanted the land for nonnative settlers. Reservations were a way of controlling the Native population. They were first created in the United States in 1851 with the Indian Appropriations Act. Many were far from a nation's traditional home.

In 1984, the Puyallup sued the U.S. government over land taken from them in 1950, and they won. On June 21, 1989, President George H. W. Bush signed the Puyallup Settlement Act. This gave the nation money for the land taken. The nation uses the money for educational, social, and economic programs.

The Puyallup Nation is one of the largest employers in Pierce County, Washington. It owns a chain of **casinos**. The nation also invests in real estate and gas stations. It built the Chinook Landing Marina to create jobs and revenue.

People once depended on waterways to provide salmon, trout, and shellfish for food. Dams and commercial fishing dropped fish populations dramatically. Now, the Puyallup's hatcheries raise salmon. Puyallup and

nonnative people also work hard to restore salmon habitat.

The Puyallup Nation funds many educational programs. It runs the Chief Leschi School in the Puyallup Valley. Of the 890 students, 98 percent are Native. Native culture is part of standard lessons from reading to math. There are also drumming, singing, and dancing activities.

SAY IT			
	pants	yelabcəd	(yo-la-tsu-in)
	shirt	puʔtəd	(po-tid)
	coat	kəpu	(ke-poh)
	hat	šiqʷ	(se-ku)

Children at the Chief Leschi School learn Puyallup traditions.

CHAPTER NINE

TSIMSHIAN

Tsimshian ceremonial mask from the 19th century

Tsimshian communities are found in northwestern British Columbia and southeast Alaska. Approximately 4,000 Tsimshian People live in Canada. Canadian Tsimshian belong to the Tsimshian First Nations. They are working out land claims with the British Columbia government.

These First Nations people live in small towns. Urban centers of Prince Rupert and Terrace also have Tsimshian populations. Many communities run successful businesses. The Lax Kw'alaams Nation is the largest Tsimshian community in Canada. The nation owns nine companies. It employs one-half of Kaien Island's Tsimshian population. The nation owns a cannery that exports fish to Asia. It also manages its forests.

Cultural and spiritual celebrations such as the potlatch were once banned by the Canadian and U.S. federal governments. At a potlatch, the host gave gifts, and food was shared with guests. Governments wanted Native Peoples to give up their beliefs and practices. Native activists worked to get the bans repealed. Now Native People are free to celebrate their traditions.

Approximately 1,900 Tsimshian lived in Alaska in 2010. They live in Metlakatla on Annette Island and in Ketchikan on the mainland. Tsimshian in Alaska came from British Columbia. They converted to Christianity and followed a missionary to Alaska in 1887. He was forming a new church. Metlakatla is the only reservation in Alaska. A council of 12 elected members governs the reservation.

Traditionally, the Tsimshian economy was based on fishing, hunting, and harvesting plants. People made weapons, clothing,

SAY IT		
dog	haas	(haas)
salmon	hoon	(hawn)
cat	duus	(doos)
seal	üüla	(eu-la)

and dishes from cedar trees, roots, hides, fur, and horns. Today, hydroelectric plants harness energy from the water. People harvest seafood, including salmon and halibut. The Tsimshian-owned packing plant AIPCO processes the catch. Rich wildlife and beautiful scenery attract many tourists.

The traditional Tsimshian language is Sm'algyax. There are now few fluent speakers, but communities are taking steps to bring the language back. In Canada, Tsimshian communities offer language classes. The University of British Columbia has an online learning guide. In Alaska, the Sealaska Heritage Institute sponsors classes at different levels.

Tsimshian dancers parade during the annual Celebration festival in Juneau, Alaska.

archaeologists (ahr-kee-OL-uh-jists) Archaeologists are people who study people and cultures from long ago. Archaeologists work with Native Peoples to understand ancient artifacts.

casinos (cah-SEEN-ohs) Casinos are businesses where visitors go to play games of chance for money. Many Native Nations run casinos to make money and provide jobs for their members.

eulachon (EU-la-shon) An eulachon is a type of fish from the northeastern Pacific. Eulachon are oily fish.

First Nations (FURST NAY-shuhns) First Nations is the term is used for Native People in Canada. There are 617 First Nations communities in Canada.

harpoons (hahr-POONS) Harpoons are long spears used to hunt whales. The Makah use harpoons on whale hunts.

hydroelectric (hahy-droh-i-LEK-trik) Hydroelectric energy is energy harnessed from falling water. Dams across rivers provide hydroelectric power.

immunity (ih-MYOO-ni-tee) Immunity is a body's ability to defend itself against germs and stay healthy. Native Peoples had little immunity to new European diseases such as smallpox.

longhouses (LAWNG-hous-iz) Longhouses are homes where several families lived. The Haida People lived in longhouses.

nations (NAY-shuhns) Nations are groups or bands of Native Peoples that share a common culture and tradition. Several nations come together to hold the Celebration festival in Alaska.

oral history (AWR-uhl HIS-tuh-ree) An oral history is the history and memories of a people told out loud. An oral history might tell how Native Peoples came to live on their lands.

peninsula (puh-NIN-suh-luh) A peninsula is a piece of land that sticks out into the ocean. The Makah live on the Olympic Peninsula.

petroglyphs (PET-ruh-glifs) Petroglyphs are carvings made in rock. Ancient Native Peoples left petroglyphs on rocks.

reservations (rez-er-VAY-shuhns) Reservations are areas of land set aside for Native use. Reservations are run by their own governments and provide services to their residents.

residential schools (rez-i-DEN-shuhl SKOOLS) Residential schools were boarding schools funded by the Canadian or American federal governments for Native children. Until the middle of the 20th century, many Native children were forced to go to residential schools.

salmon run (SAM-uhn RUN) In the spring, the salmon run is the salmon migration from the ocean to the rivers where they were born. The salmon run each year was a key food source for Native Peoples of the Northwest Coast.

sovereign (SAHV-ruhn) Something that is sovereign is independent. Native Nations recognized by the government are sovereign and can control their own internal affairs.

thunderbird (THUHN-der-burd) The thunderbird is a mythical bird. The thunderbird hunts sea mammals in Pacific Coast oral histories.

TO LEARN MORE

BOOKS

Kavin, Kim, and Beth Hetland. *Native Americans: Discover The History & Cultures of the First Americans with 15 Projects.* White River Junction, VT: Nomad Press, 2013.

Nault, Jennifer. *Canadian Aboriginal Art and Culture: Haida.* New York: Weigl Publishing, 2007.

Silvey, Diane. *The Kids Book of Aboriginal Peoples in Canada.* Vancouver, BC: Kids Can Press, 2012.

WEB SITES

Visit our Web site for links about Native Nations of the Northwest Coast: **childsworld.com/links**

Note to Parents, Teachers, and Librarians: We routinely verify our Web links to make sure they are safe and active sites. So encourage your readers to check them out!